-L-I-K-

WORDS

CAN YOU MAKE THE LINK?

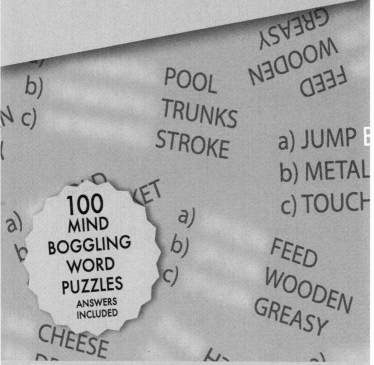

POOL
TRUNKS
STROKE

GREASY
WOODEN
FEED

a) JUMP
b) METAL
c) TOUCH

100 MIND BOGGLING WORD PUZZLES
ANSWERS INCLUDED

a)
b)
c)

FEED
WOODEN
GREASY

CHEESE

Find the letters that can be placed before or after the words given in each question to make a new word or phrase

First published in 2016 by
Clarity Media Ltd
www.clarity-media.co.uk

Puzzles created by Dan Moore
Design and layout by Amy Smith

About Clarity Media

Clarity Media are a leading provider of a huge range of puzzles for adults and children. For more information on our services, please visit us at www.pzle.co.uk. For information on purchasing puzzles for publication, visit us at www.clarity-media.co.uk

Puzzle Magazines

If you enjoy the puzzles in this book, then you may be interested in our puzzle magazines. We have a very large range of magazines that you can download and print yourself in PDF format at our Puzzle Magazine site. For more information, take a look at www.puzzle-magazine.com

Online Puzzles

If you prefer to play puzzles online, please take a look at the Puzzle Club website at www.thepuzzleclub.com

For more puzzle books visit
WWW.PUZZLE-BOOK.CO.UK

CONTENTS

....

Welcome to this mind-boggling collection of 100 link word questions. The rules are simple but the challenges are sure to test your knowledge! Find the letters that can be placed before or after the words given in each question to make a new word or phrase. The length of letters in the word is given as a clue for each question.

An example is shown below:

Q) Can you find the 6-letter word that can be placed either before or after the following three words to make a new word or phrase?

a) TABLE
b) CUP
c) BREAK

A) COFFEE

1) Can you find the 4-letter word that can be placed either before or after the following three words to make a new word or phrase?

a) BED   *TWIN*
b) EVIL
c) IDENTICAL

2) Can you find the 6-letter word that can be placed either before or after the following three words to make a new word or phrase?

a) BULL
b) FREE
c) BLACK

3) Can you find the 8-letter word that can be placed either before or after the following three words to make a new word or phrase?

a) POOL   *SWIMMING*
b) TRUNKS
c) STROKE

4) Can you find the 5-letter word that can be placed either before or after the following three words to make a new word or phrase?

a) BREAD   *Quick*
b) FIX
c) DOUBLE

5) Can you find the 5-letter word that can be placed either before or after the following three words to make a new word or phrase?

a) LEVEL
b) POINT   *Entry*
c) DATA

6) Can you find the 5-letter word that can be placed either before or after the following three words to make a new word or phrase?

a) ACTION
b) STRUGGLE
c) ECONOMY

7) Can you find the 6-letter word that can be placed either before or after the following three words to make a new word or phrase?

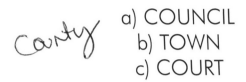
Canty

a) COUNCIL
b) TOWN
c) COURT

8) Can you find the 4-letter word that can be placed either before or after the following three words to make a new word or phrase?

a) PERFECT
b) SQUARE
c) LOAN

9) Can you find the 6-letter word that can be placed either before or after the following three words to make a new word or phrase?

a) DATING
b) COPY
c) CYCLE

6

10) Can you find the 5-letter word that can be placed either before or after the following three words to make a new word or phrase?

Spoon

a) FEED
b) WOODEN
c) GREASY

11) Can you find the 4-letter word that can be placed either before or after the following three words to make a new word or phrase?

a) CHORUS
b) SERVICE
c) PARTY

12) Can you find the 6-letter word that can be placed either before or after the following three words to make a new word or phrase?

a) BAND
b) STAMP
c) TREE

13) Can you find the 7-letter word that can be placed either before or after the following three words to make a new word or phrase?

a) DUCK
b) ROOM
c) PRETTY

14) Can you find the 5-letter word that can be placed either before or after the following three words to make a new word or phrase?

a) CAR
b) TELEVISION
c) MODEM

15) Can you find the 4-letter word that can be placed either before or after the following three words to make a new word or phrase?

a) MOON
b) CHEESE
c) CHIP

16) Can you find the 4-letter word that can be placed either before or after the following three words to make a new word or phrase?

a) SHARP
b) AROUND
c) FORWARD

17) Can you find the 3-letter word that can be placed either before or after the following three words to make a new word or phrase?

a) BALE
b) MAKE
c) FEVER

18) Can you find the 5-letter word that can be placed either before or after the following three words to make a new word or phrase?

a) PRESSURE
b) BANK
c) BROTHER

19) Can you find the 5-letter word that can be placed either before or after the following three words to make a new word or phrase?

a) VILLAGE
b) TEA
c) BOWLING

20) Can you find the 7-letter word that can be placed either before or after the following three words to make a new word or phrase?

a) POLICE
b) EXPERIMENT
c) SECOND

21) Can you find the 6-letter word that can be placed either before or after the following three words to make a new word or phrase?

a) CRAB
b) MONKEY
c) PLANT

22) Can you find the 7-letter word that can be placed either before or after the following three words to make a new word or phrase?

a) GUN
b) JACKET
c) ROOM

23) Can you find the 4-letter word that can be placed either before or after the following three words to make a new word or phrase?

a) TRACK
b) FOOD
c) FORWARD

24) Can you find the 3-letter word that can be placed either before or after the following three words to make a new word or phrase?

a) OLD
b) BRACKET
c) LIMIT

25) Can you find the 5-letter word that can be placed either before or after the following three words to make a new word or phrase?

a) CRAB
b) BIG
c) TOFFEE

26) Can you find the 7-letter word that can be placed either before or after the following three words to make a new word or phrase?

a) CLASS
b) DRIVE
c) MARKET

27) Can you find the 5-letter word that can be placed either before or after the following three words to make a new word or phrase?

a) UNION
b) SECRET
c) WIND

28) Can you find the 6-letter word that can be placed either before or after the following three words to make a new word or phrase?

a) GUESS
b) NATURE
c) STRING

29) Can you find the 4-letter word that can be placed either before or after the following three words to make a new word or phrase?

a) JUMP
b) METAL
c) TOUCH

30) Can you find the 5-letter word that can be placed either before or after the following three words to make a new word or phrase?

a) FLOOR
b) HALL
c) MUSIC

31) Can you find the 4-letter word that can be placed either before or after the following three words to make a new word or phrase?

a) LANGUAGE
b) IMAGE
c) POLITIC

32) Can you find the 5-letter word that can be placed either before or after the following three words to make a new word or phrase?

a) MARKET
b) EXCHANGE
c) ROLLING

33) Can you find the 5-letter word that can be placed either before or after the following three words to make a new word or phrase?

a) HARVEST
b) FIELD
c) MAT

34) Can you find the 6-letter word that can be placed either before or after the following three words to make a new word or phrase?

a) ENGLISH
b) GROUND
c) FINGER

35) Can you find the 4-letter word that can be placed either before or after the following three words to make a new word or phrase?

a) ANGEL
b) MARBLE
c) POUND

36) Can you find the 7-letter word that can be placed either before or after the following three words to make a new word or phrase?

a) ROD
b) EXPEDITION
c) FLY

37) Can you find the 8-letter word that can be placed either before or after the following three words to make a new word or phrase?

a) BLANKET
b) SHOCK
c) CHARGE

38) Can you find the 3-letter word that can be placed either before or after the following three words to make a new word or phrase?

a) RING
b) SKELETON
c) SIGNATURE

39) Can you find the 5-letter word that can be placed either before or after the following three words to make a new word or phrase?

a) TABLE
b) ROBIN
c) TRIP

40) Can you find the 4-letter word that can be placed either before or after the following three words to make a new word or phrase?

a) FACE
b) SKI
c) DEAD

41) Can you find the 5-letter word that can be placed either before or after the following three words to make a new word or phrase?

a) STATION
b) PLAY
c) PLANT

42) Can you find the 8-letter word that can be placed either before or after the following three words to make a new word or phrase?

a) CASE
b) PLAN
c) CYCLE

43) Can you find the 4-letter word that can be placed either before or after the following three words to make a new word or phrase?

a) RUSH
b) COAST
c) STANDARD

44) Can you find the 8-letter word that can be placed either before or after the following three words to make a new word or phrase?

a) CHEESE
b) DREAM
c) FOOTBALL

45) Can you find the 5-letter word that can be placed either before or after the following three words to make a new word or phrase?

a) HALL
b) BOX
c) FOLK

46) Can you find the 7-letter word that can be placed either before or after the following three words to make a new word or phrase?

a) SPORT
b) TENNIS
c) SQUASH

47) Can you find the 4-letter word that can be placed either before or after the following three words to make a new word or phrase?

a) SODA
b) SANDWICH
c) COUNTRY

48) Can you find the 5-letter word that can be placed either before or after the following three words to make a new word or phrase?

a) SYSTEM
b) WIND
c) PANEL

49) Can you find the 5-letter word that can be placed either before or after the following three words to make a new word or phrase?

a) MOTHER
b) ALKALINE
c) RARE

50) Can you find the 5-letter word that can be placed either before or after the following three words to make a new word or phrase?

a) SAUCE
b) KNIFE
c) BIN

51) Can you find the 4-letter word that can be placed either before or after the following three words to make a new word or phrase?

a) PRESSURE
b) GROUP
c) REVIEW

52) Can you find the 6-letter word that can be placed either before or after the following three words to make a new word or phrase?

a) HEART
b) ROYAL
c) PATCH

53) Can you find the 5-letter word that can be placed either before or after the following three words to make a new word or phrase?

a) BULLET
b) SQUARE
c) CARPET

54) Can you find the 4-letter word that can be placed either before or after the following three words to make a new word or phrase?

a) SOLDIER
b) BRAKE
c) TRAFFIC

55) Can you find the 4-letter word that can be placed either before or after the following three words to make a new word or phrase?

a) STOP
b) CIRCLE
c) TIME

56) Can you find the 5-letter word that can be placed either before or after the following three words to make a new word or phrase?

a) MOB
b) FLOOD
c) POINT

57) Can you find the 4-letter word that can be placed either before or after the following three words to make a new word or phrase?

a) NAME
b) SOURCE
c) DRESS

58) Can you find the 5-letter word that can be placed either before or after the following three words to make a new word or phrase?

a) SCRAP
b) HEAVY
c) BASE

59) Can you find the 6-letter word that can be placed either before or after the following three words to make a new word or phrase?

a) PUPPET
b) GRAND
c) PAST

60) Can you find the 4-letter word that can be placed either before or after the following three words to make a new word or phrase?

a) PONY
b) BUSINESS
c) TRIAL

23

61) Can you find the 6-letter word that can be placed either before or after the following three words to make a new word or phrase?

a) ROCK
b) BELL
c) LINE

62) Can you find the 3-letter word that can be placed either before or after the following three words to make a new word or phrase?

a) LUCK
b) ROAST
c) COFFEE

63) Can you find the 6-letter word that can be placed either before or after the following three words to make a new word or phrase?

a) ERROR
b) SOLAR
c) DIGESTIVE

64) Can you find the 3-letter word that can be placed either before or after the following three words to make a new word or phrase?

a) EVIL
b) COMPOUND
c) CATCHING

65) Can you find the 4-letter word that can be placed either before or after the following three words to make a new word or phrase?

a) SUPPORT
b) VEST
c) SCIENCE

66) Can you find the 5-letter word that can be placed either before or after the following three words to make a new word or phrase?

a) INSIDE
b) FAST
c) RECORD

67) Can you find the 5-letter word that can be placed either before or after the following three words to make a new word or phrase?

a) MARTIAL
b) ORDER
c) KANGAROO

68) Can you find the 5-letter word that can be placed either before or after the following three words to make a new word or phrase?

a) WORSHIP
b) HOLY
c) BELT

69) Can you find the 4-letter word that can be placed either before or after the following three words to make a new word or phrase?

a) CARBON
b) HARD
c) PROTECTION

70) Can you find the 4-letter word that can be placed either before or after the following three words to make a new word or phrase?

a) VARIABLE
b) MORNING
c) ROCK

71) Can you find the 6-letter word that can be placed either before or after the following three words to make a new word or phrase?

a) PLAYER
b) BREAKER
c) TRACK

72) Can you find the 5-letter word that can be placed either before or after the following three words to make a new word or phrase?

a) WORLD
b) DEGREE
c) PARTY

73) Can you find the 3-letter word that can be placed either before or after the following three words to make a new word or phrase?

a) OFFICE
b) SEAT
c) SHADOW

74) Can you find the 4-letter word that can be placed either before or after the following three words to make a new word or phrase?

a) MINUTE
b) STRAW
c) RESORT

75) Can you find the 6-letter word that can be placed either before or after the following three words to make a new word or phrase?

a) SENSE
b) LAW
c) GROUND

76) Can you find the 4-letter word that can be placed either before or after the following three words to make a new word or phrase?

a) TURKEY
b) FEET
c) WAR

77) Can you find the 3-letter word that can be placed either before or after the following three words to make a new word or phrase?

a) CHEST
b) CRIME
c) PAINT

78) Can you find the 7-letter word that can be placed either before or after the following three words to make a new word or phrase?

a) SECTOR
b) DETECTIVE
c) EYE

79) Can you find the 4-letter word that can be placed either before or after the following three words to make a new word or phrase?

a) EARTH
b) BREED
c) MEDIUM

80) Can you find the 4-letter word that can be placed either before or after the following three words to make a new word or phrase?

a) BIT
b) SPARE
c) TAKE

81) Can you find the 5-letter word that can be placed either before or after the following three words to make a new word or phrase?

a) KNIFE
b) HOUSE
c) RUMP

82) Can you find the 4-letter word that can be placed either before or after the following three words to make a new word or phrase?

a) SHOPPING
b) GOLF
c) AWAY

83) Can you find the 7-letter word that can be placed either before or after the following three words to make a new word or phrase?

a) BIG
b) BLOOD
c) HALF

84) Can you find the 6-letter word that can be placed either before or after the following three words to make a new word or phrase?

a) COUCH
b) JACKET
c) SALAD

85) Can you find the 4-letter word that can be placed either before or after the following three words to make a new word or phrase?

a) JACKET
b) CLUB
c) ORDER

86) Can you find the 5-letter word that can be placed either before or after the following three words to make a new word or phrase?

a) DECISION
b) CUP
c) COUNTDOWN

87) Can you find the 5-letter word that can be placed either before or after the following three words to make a new word or phrase?

a) EFFECT
b) WAVE
c) SYSTEM

88) Can you find the 7-letter word that can be placed either before or after the following three words to make a new word or phrase?

a) INSTANT
b) TEXT
c) BOARD

89) Can you find the 10-letter word that can be placed either before or after the following three words to make a new word or phrase?

a) POCKET
b) DEFINITION
c) ENTRY

90) Can you find the 4-letter word that can be placed either before or after the following three words to make a new word or phrase?

a) CERTIFICATE
b) SHOP
c) WRAP

91) Can you find the 4-letter word that can be placed either before or after the following three words to make a new word or phrase?

a) HIRED
b) DOMESTIC
c) DESK

92) Can you find the 6-letter word that can be placed either before or after the following three words to make a new word or phrase?

a) TABLE
b) CUP
c) BREAK

93) Can you find the 5-letter word that can be placed either before or after the following three words to make a new word or phrase?

a) NOISE
b) ELEPHANT
c) GOLD

94) Can you find the 5-letter word that can be placed either before or after the following three words to make a new word or phrase?

a) COLD
b) AGE
c) BROKE

95) Can you find the 4-letter word that can be placed either before or after the following three words to make a new word or phrase?

a) BRAKE
b) LUGGAGE
c) WHIP

96) Can you find the 3-letter word that can be placed either before or after the following three words to make a new word or phrase?

a) ACTOR
b) RADIO
c) HOCK

97) Can you find the 4-letter word that can be placed either before or after the following three words to make a new word or phrase?

a) BERTH
b) EYED
c) AWAKE

98) Can you find the 4-letter word that can be placed either before or after the following three words to make a new word or phrase?

a) CHECK
b) BLIND
c) BEAUTY

99) Can you find the 4-letter word that can be placed either before or after the following three words to make a new word or phrase?

a) TEA
b) BAY
c) FIG

100) Can you find the 6-letter word that can be placed either before or after the following three words to make a new word or phrase?

a) BUBBLE
b) FREE
c) RECOGNITION

ANSWERS:

1) TWIN
2) MARKET
3) SWIMMING
4) QUICK
5) ENTRY
6) CLASS
7) COUNTY
8) WORD
9) CARBON
10) SPOON
11) LINE
12) RUBBER
13) SITTING
14) CABLE
15) BLUE
16) LOOK
17) HAY
18) BLOOD
19) GREEN
20) THOUGHT
21) SPIDER
22) SMOKING
23) FAST
24) AGE

25) APPLE
26) ECONOMY
27) TRADE
28) SECOND
29) BASE
30) DANCE
31) BODY
32) STOCK
33) MOUSE
34) MIDDLE
35) CAKE
36) FISHING
37) ELECTRIC
38) KEY
39) ROUND
40) LIFT
41) POWER
42) BUSINESS
43) GOLD
44) AMERICAN
45) MUSIC
46) RACQUET
47) CLUB
48) SOLAR
49) EARTH
50) BREAD

51) PEER
52) PURPLE
53) MAGIC
54) FOOT
55) FULL
56) FLASH
57) CODE
58) METAL
59) MASTER
60) SHOW
61) BOTTOM
62) POT
63) SYSTEM
64) EYE
65) LIFE
66) TRACK
67) COURT
68) BIBLE
69) COPY
70) STAR
71) RECORD
72) THIRD
73) BOX
74) LAST
75) COMMON
76) COLD

77) WAR
78) PRIVATE
79) RARE
80) PART
81) STEAK
82) CART
83) BROTHER
84) POTATO
85) BOOK
86) FINAL
87) SOUND
88) MESSAGE
89) DICTIONARY
90) GIFT
91) HELP
92) COFFEE
93) WHITE
94) STONE
95) HAND
96) HAM
97) WIDE
98) SPOT
99) LEAF
100) SPEECH

Printed in Great Britain
by Amazon